The Ultimate Truth
About Love & Happiness

by Lester Levenson

A Handbook to Life

Publisher:
        Lawrence Crane Enterprises, Inc.
        15101 Rayneta Drive
        Sherman Oaks, CA 91403
        Phone: 888-333-7703 or 818-385-0611
        Fax: 818-385-0563
        Email: ReleaseLA@aol.com
        Web site: www.releasetechnique.com

ISBN No. 09711755351795

Printed in the United States of America

Library of Congress number TX5-021-629

The publisher and author of this material make no medical claims for its use. This material is not intended to treat, diagnose or cure any illness. If you need medical attention please consult with your medical practitioner.

FOREWORD

"The only method of receiving love is to give love,

because what we give out must come back."

Lester Levenson was born in Elizabeth, New Jersey, on July 19, 1909.

Lester sailed through school and college with astonishing ease, becoming a physicist, an engineer, a successful businessman and a self-made millionaire. Yet despite all his achievements there was an innate turmoil in his heart, an anxiety and stress that seemed to rule his life.

In 1952, at the age of 42, Lester had his second massive heart attack. In those days, they did not have bypass surgery or heart transplants and so when he came out of the emergency room, the doctors told him, "Lester, we're sorry to tell you, but you have two weeks to live, three at the most, and we can't do anything for you. So we're sending you home."

So Lester went home.

Being a physicist, he knew he had to go back to the drawing board, wipe the slate clean, and start from point zero. So he started to examine his life. He noticed that each time he was ill he was wanting something and that the intense wanting feelings were what was actually making him miserable. He wanted love, he wanted money, he wanted to change things, and every time he looked at that wanting, he had an uncomfortable feeling that he traced back to his illness. Then he noticed that whenever he was giving and loving and wasn't wanting anything, he was not ill. So, he asked himself, "Well, if I could get rid of all my non-loving feelings, would I get better?" He thought about this question and uncovered something that was startling to him at the time.

He noticed that when he was loving he was happiest. That happiness equated to being loving rather than being loved.

> *HE NOTICED THAT WHEN HE WAS LOVING HE WAS HAPPIEST. THAT HAPPINESS EQUATED TO BEING LOVING RATHER THAN BEING LOVED.*

That was a starting point. He asked himself if he could cure his illnesses this way. So, he began connecting all of his thoughts and feelings in that direction—from that of "wanting to be loved," to that of "loving." He examined all his relationships and he let go of all of his non-loving feelings from the past. In that process he made another shocking discovery: He saw that he wanted to change the entire world and that was the cause of all his ailments, making him a slave to this world. He decided to reverse that by actually unloading the subconscious concepts and pressures, and by taking responsibility for everything happening in his life. At this point he discovered that limitations were only concepts in our minds and can easily be dropped. He realized that God is within us all, that we are infinite beings with no limitations. With that realization, he became happier: freer, lighter and with an overall sense of well-being.

Later on he would say: "We are all gods acting like goddamned fools."

Months went by and Lester still wasn't dead. He hardly went to sleep, he ate a little bit, and he continued to work on himself. He corrected his physical body. All of his miseries dropped away and he found himself in a place in which he was happy all the time, without sorrow. He totally cured himself.

More than that, Lester unlocked the science of the mind: How the mind works, what to do about it and how to correct it. How to correct your thinking. How to call up the menu of your mind, take a look at this menu and eliminate what you don't want.

Lester was a giving person—one thousand percent! He spent the remainder of his life helping others discover this secret that he had unlocked for himself. He passed on in 1994 at the age of 84—42 years after being told he had two to three weeks to live!

And before he died, he asked me to continue his work.

My name is Larry Crane. I was born in the Bronx. I grew up in a poor family. We never missed a meal, but I thought the rich man lived on the top floor and the poor man lived in the basement. And we lived in the basement. As a young boy, I had many, many jobs; I was very aggressive. I worked hard, put myself through New York University, The Leonard Stern School of Business, and when I graduated college in 1957, my father told me if I could make $100 a week, it would be a terrific accomplishment. I noticed some of my friends who graduated started to be successful and were making lots of money, so I said to myself, "I'm just as smart as they are. I can do that, too." So I went about life and business in a very aggressive way, like "Get outta my way—I'll take what I want—I'm gonna have what I want or I'll knock you down." And in time, I climbed my way to the top.

During that period I got married and had twin sons but never made any time for them. I started in the advertising business and quickly became the advertising and marketing director of Remco Toys. After a few very successful years, I started my own direct mail business, Telehouse, Inc., which was the first of its kind to sell record packages on television. The company quickly became very successful. We started to make millions of dollars. I divorced my first wife and married a beautiful, beautiful woman. I bought a ten-room duplex penthouse in Manhattan. I had the limousines, the planes—I had businesses all over the world making multi-millions. Yet, I was absolutely miserable!

It was quite confusing to me. One night I came home to my fabulous ten-room Manhattan penthouse apartment. <u>Time</u> magazine had written an article about me, and the doorman greeted me with, "Mr. Crane, what an honor to have you in my building. For me to take you up to your penthouse is my pleasure." This was a Friday night around 9 p.m. and I remember getting out of the elevator and being so unhappy and so miserable that I actually walked over to the terrace and for about two hours I contemplated jumping—ending it all. I call this the second greatest day of my life! (The first: Meeting Lester Levenson). But that Friday evening I, too, examined my life. I asked myself what am I doing on the planet? What is life about? I observed that I did not know what I was doing on Earth, but for me life was only about making money. I was so focused on money that I did not even allow myself to spend much, enjoy much or do much with it. That was confusing. I decided that evening to find an answer. After all, I had no reason to be miserable: I had millions of dollars, a beautiful wife, a fabulous business, businesses all over the world, media attention, and so on and so forth. Still, I was miserable. I was not interested in drugs or drinking. These things had no appeal to me and thank God I never turned in that direction. Since I was not willing to jump and end it, I needed to find an answer.

At the time, I was not receptive to psychiatric work. I was not open to transcendental meditation or yoga. I was pretty closed in those days and yet I wasn't willing to jump. So I became determined to find an answer. What that answer was, I did not know. My wife at the time talked me into some New Age courses, which I took, but I still found no answer after taking a number of them and trying to put an end to my unhappiness. I tried and tried, but I did not have the answer that I wanted. All I really wanted was to get out of my misery. I discovered I was angry. I discovered I had fear. I discovered I was doing things that were destructive and not quite intelligent behavior, yet I didn't know what to do about it. None of the courses showed me what to do about it. I just became more and more frustrated. I then took some additional courses, but still to no avail.

Then one day, in 1976, a man came into my office to sell me a mail order item. I had some interesting spiritual or self-discipline quotations on my office wall which often opened up a conversation of what I was into and the answers I was seeking. This salesman told me about "The Release® Technique." It really resonated with me, so I decided to take the course that very weekend. That same weekend, I met Lester Levenson, my mentor, my teacher, who I was fortunate enough to know for twenty-two years. I spoke to him almost every day, many times during the day. I took trips with him around the country and was quite fascinated by his clarity, his calmness and his givingness.

Now let's talk about what people are looking for—what everyone is looking for—and how to get it.

Everyone is looking for "happiness with no sorrow" or peace of mind, but most people are looking for this outside themselves. They are looking for it in someone, in some thing, in making money, being a big shot, having possessions. Unfortunately, it is impossible to find peace of mind that way. Take it for checking. Take a look at somebody who is powerful, who is monetarily successful. How happy are they? How satisfied are they? Do they really have peace of mind?

Let's take a look at those individuals who are trying to get happiness and peace of mind from a relationship. Does that relationship give peace of mind? Take a check and see if you have happiness with no sorrow, peace of mind, and where you are looking of it. Are you seeking it in a person who is unhappy or relatively unhappy? You must go inside yourself in order to find peace of mind and happiness. By unloading your limitations, you will discover that you are already unlimited and you can do anything you want. Just unload your limiting thoughts.

Peace of mind means a quiet mind, not a noisy mind. That is why only a few of us ever find it. We are looking for peace of mind outside ourselves and peace of mind can only be acquired by having a quiet mind. The more one quiets his or her mind, the more powerful one becomes. That is what we are going to explore.

Before sending you on to explore this rich territory with Lester, there are a few suggestions which may help you on your journey. Each of the talks you are about to read is designed to bring a key theme into your awareness. Each also represents not only thoughts for your mind to digest, but more importantly, energy for your whole being to absorb. Because of this, Lester recommends that you not hurdle your way through them. Instead, read them slowly, allowing enough time for reflection and integration. In short, approach this material as you would a private talk with a good friend. Approach it with an open heart and mind and allow it to deliver its gifts to you. Above all, by working slowly with this material you will give yourself the opportunity to practice many of the powerful and practical tools it contains. If you do this honestly and persistently, you will give yourself the opportunity to practice many of the powerful and practical tools it contains. If you do this honestly and persistently, you will give yourself a gift of inestimable value. You will discover for yourself a direct link to the source of your own wisdom. You will, as Lester so often says, "come to know that you know." And this, after all, is the ultimate goal of any true teaching.

Finally, it is important for you to know that these sessions are designed to give you a great deal more than a different intellectual perspective on the human condition. For as our guide says repeatedly in the following pages—"thinking will not get you there." Instead, this material, the questions and answers, the aphorisms, and the suggested exercises are all intended as an introduction to a remarkable, experiential process that is as simple, as clear and as powerful as the words themselves. This process is called the "Release Technique," and it is, quite simply put, a very direct, easy to use way to eliminate the boundaries of thoughts, feelings, emotions and wants which stand between you and self-realization.

So after you have spent time in these sessions, I encourage you to turn to the material in Appendix A and introduce yourself to this innovative transformation technique which Lester discovered on his journey to personal realization. Through it I believe you will discover a key to achieving the quality of life and consciousness you seek. And I know that through a loving and committed practice of it you will experience that unlimited, joyous and powerful state of being that is our natural right and our natural state.

I wish you a remarkable and joyful adventure.

Love,

Larry Crane

The Ultimate Truth About Love & Happiness

CONTENTS

PAGE

Introduction 1

The Basic Goal 3

Happiness—What Is It? 5

Love—What Is It? 7

Peace—What Is It? 13

Truth—What Is It? 14

The Self (God)—What Is It? 16

How to Help Others 18

Teacher of Truth—How To Find One 27

The Ego—What Is It? 30

The Mind—What Is It? 33

Lester on Demonstration 38

The World 41

Sex and Marriage 45

Desire—What Is It? 49

Emotion—What Is It? 51

Pleasure/Pain—What Is It? 54

Health and Supply—How To Get It 56

Spiritual Growth—What Is It? 59

Releasing 62

Practical Methods That May Be Used Daily 63

Ways of Getting Out of a Blue Mood
into a Happy Mood 66

Different Paths—How To Get There 67

Thoughts 68

Self-Growth Yardsticks 82

Law of Compensation or Karma 83

A Summary
The Self-God-Absolute Truth 84

Lester in His Own Words 88

A Message from Lester 93

INTRODUCTION

The Ultimate Truth is Truth that is true now, has always been true, and will forever be true.

Man cannot make this Truth nor can he change this Truth. He can only discover it. He may choose to live in accord with it. If he so does, he finds himself supremely happy beyond anything he could imagine! All limitations drop away and he discovers that all power, all knowledge, and all joy are his and that all this is his natural, inherent state.

A unique characteristic of this Truth is that it must be seen by each one through his own perception. No one and no book can do it for him. Teachers and books (scriptures) can only point out the direction, the way, and the individual may choose to take it.

Necessary is the proof of Truth, and necessary it is that each one must prove the Truth for himself. Nothing should ever be accepted on hearsay. One should listen to, reflect upon, and then prove. The best attitude one may take would be to not believe nor disbelieve, but to accept Truths for checking. Then, and only then, after one has proven them without a doubt should one accept them.

As Truth begins to prove itself, one gains more confidence in it, and then proofs come more easily and more readily; until finally, one perceives the Absolute Truth—that we are unlimited beings, unlimited in our knowledge, power and joy.

We must start from where we are, so we start with thinking in the realm of thinkingness. Then we progress to a stage of thought—feelings where thoughts have feeling to them. This continues until there is only feelingness. When this becomes the basis for our actions, we are intuitive and in tune with the world. Finally, there is only the realm of beingness, and in this state we perceive ourselves as being the All, and we see no-otherness.

Beginning with thought, we direct our minds towards thoughts that will free us; liberate us from sorrow and unhappiness. This leads to happiness, which is in the realm of feelingness. When the feeling of happiness is developed fully, there is only happiness of being, and we then enter into the state of exalted bliss, tranquility and serenity.

The time required to accomplish this varies widely. The quickness of one's understanding is directly proportional to the intensity of one's desire for truth.

All authoritarianism is let go of, as the only authority for Truth is Truth and not man. In place of authority is given the dictum—"Prove it yourself." Only when proven for oneself does one have it and can one use it. One knows only that which he can do.

The ultimate Truth is not the usual. If something should offend, shock, or challenge, it is suggested that you check into it, as the chances are that a fixed concept might be needing reevaluation; that by doing so you might find yourself a bit freer.

Lester Levenson

THE BASIC GOAL

The goal is unlimited happiness with no sorrow.

The goal is complete liberation—the attainment of limitlessness.

All are seeking complete freedom and happiness, and everyone is seeking this either consciously or unconsciously.

The goal is Self-Realization.

HAPPINESS—WHAT IS IT?

The only place where we can feel happiness is right within ourselves.

> **"HAPPINESS IS EQUAL TO ONE'S CAPACITY TO LOVE."**

Happiness is our inherent, natural state.

Happiness is you being you without any negativity.

The best definition for happiness is peace, tranquility, and serenity.

Every being is seeking freedom and the complete freedom or liberation is also the ultimate happiness.

Happiness is the absence of apathy, grief, fear, jealousy, anger, and hate.

There isn't anyone who is not seeking it.

Happiness loves.

The only place where we can feel happiness is right within ourselves.

Happiness is freedom; absence of limitations. The less limited we are, the freer we are—the happier we are.

Happiness is equal to one's capacity to love.

Happiness is keeping in mind the things we do want.

The happiness with no sorrow "can only be found by going within."

Unhappiness is keeping in mind the things we do not want.

If we love completely, we are perfectly happy.

Happiness is being cause rather than effect; master rather than victim.

Love equals happiness. When we are not happy, we are not loving.

Happiness involves thoughts of oneness; unhappiness, thoughts of separation.

Happiness that we are seeking is nothing but our very own self, our very own beingness.

Happiness thinks of thou, with no ego motivation; unhappiness, I, with ego motivation.

The only way we can be happy is to let go of all desires, than we become perfectly content.

Happiness is calmness with no emotion or effort; unhappiness involves energy, emotion, and effort.

An attitude of giving makes one happy.

Joy is in the spirit of giving.

LOVE—WHAT IS IT?

Love is a feeling of givingness with no thought of receiving any return for it.

> **LOVE BEGETS LOVE**

Love is allowing the other person to have exactly what they want, even though you cannot give it to them.

Love is giving with no strings attached.

Love is the natural, inherent state of man.

Only by loving does love come to us. The more we love, the more love comes to us.

Love and giving are two words that are synonymous.

Love is an attitude, a feeling, and requires no action.

Love is a freeing of the other one.

Love is acceptance.

The more we develop love, the more we come in touch with harmony of the universe, the more delightful our life becomes, the more beautiful, the more everything. It starts a cycle going in which you spin upward.

Love is taking people as they are.

Love is loving the other one because the other one is the way the other one is.

Love is only understood when you love.

Love is trust.

When you love fully, you understand the other one fully.

Love is a feelingness of peace.

Love is identification. It is being the other one by identifying with the other one.

Love is what every being is seeking through his every act.

Love is the answer to all problems.

When there are problems, if we would love more, they would disappear. When the love is complete, the problem dissolves immediately.

Love and understanding are the same.

Love is communing; it is communication.

Lending support, wanting for the other one what the other one wants, that is love.

The greatest help or giving one may give to another is to help the other to get the understanding of Truth. In this way, one gives the other the formula for happiness.

Love is a power. It is the cohesive force of the universe.

Love is attracting, integrating, and constructive and so affects anything that it is applied to.

Parliaments cannot right the world; but enough individuals feeling love can.

Almost all people mistake ego approval for love. Because it is not love, it is not satisfying. Consequently, one continuously needs and demands it. And this produces only frustration.

Love is not sex.

Love is not an emotion.

People need each other and think it is love. There's no hanging on to, or fencing in, of the other one when one loves.

Human love does not want to share its love with others, but rather wants its own personal satisfaction. Real love wants to share its love and the more it is shared, the more joyous it is.

There is no "longing for" in love, because longing is separation; love being oneness, it does not allow separation.

True love cannot be gotten through marriage. It must be there before marriage.

Love cannot be applied to one and not another. It's impossible to love one and hate another. When we love one more than another, that one is doing something for us. That is human love. When one loves people because they are nice to him, that too, is human love. True love is unconditional. In true love, one loves even those who oppose him.

We should love everyone equally.

It's impossible to get love. Only by loving can one feel love.

The more one looks for love, the more one doesn't love.

One should strive to love, never to be loved. To be loved brings temporary happiness, ego inflation.

When one loves fully, one can have no concept of not being loved.

To love our enemy is the height of love.

When love is felt for the enemy, it makes the enemy impotent; powerless to hurt us. If the enemy persists in trying to hurt us, he will only hurt himself.

One does not increase his love. One merely gets rid of one's hate.

In a state of high love one has a feeling of harmlessness, and grants the other one the other one's beingness.

When we love fully, we feel we have everything.

Loving fully, one sees only love.

When one really loves, one can never be hurt.

Love has no personal angles.

Anytime one feels good, one is loving. Anytime one feels bad, one is not loving.

Love and egoism are opposites.

Love is selflessness.

Love is purity.

Love eliminates fear.

Love eliminates anxiety.

Love eliminates insecurity.

Love eliminates loneliness.

Love eliminates unhappiness.

Love attracts love.

Love is the means and the end.

Love is its own reward.

Love seeks its own likeness.

Love flourishes in love.

Love is contagious.

Love cannot be intellectualized.

The sweetness of love cannot be described. It must be experienced.

Full love is constant and can never be not. When attained, one feels only it, sees only it, hears only it, and thinks only it.

Love is patient and kind. Love is not jealous or boastful. It is not arrogant or rude. Love does not insist on its own way. It is not irritable or resentful. It does not rejoice at wrong, but rejoices in the right. Love bears all things, believes all things, hopes all things, endures all things.

PEACE—WHAT IS IT?

Peace is tranquility, serenity, and is a dwelling in the Self.

Complete peace is our highest state and is the natural state.

Peace is dwelling in the realm of all knowledge and all beauty in complete harmony.

> REAL LOVE, DIVINE LOVE, IS A FEELING OF GIVINGNESS WITH NO EXPECTATIONS OF RECEIVING SOMETHING FOR IT IN RETURN.

Peace is at-onement, no-otherness.

Peace is non-resistance, complete acceptance, identification with all, everyone, everything.

Peace is a feeling and requires no action.

Peace is in the realm of Beingness.

Complete peace is impossible in the realm of thought. Thoughts agitate. There must be no thought to have perfect and total peace.

In oneness, there is no other to think about.

Peace is the best indication of one's state, and may be used as a measure to gauge one's progress.

When one is in the quiet, peace shows itself in the freedom from unwanted thoughts, and in the ability to concentrate on a single thought.

TRUTH—WHAT IS IT?

Truth is That which never changes. All else is untrue, illusion, and apparency.

The greatest thing we can give is wisdom, because when you give one wisdom, you give not just one single thing, but you give one the method of attaining everything.

The only authority for Truth is Truth.

Truth is, regardless of people, no one can make Truth or unmake it.

Truth is the only authority for Truth.

Truth cannot be taught. It can only be discovered, realized.

One should never accept anything until he can prove it out for himself. There are two ways to prove things, externally and internally. Externally is proving it in the world by doing it. Internally is by seeing it intuitively through the omniscient part of oneself.

There is no problem which cannot be dissolved immediately in the light of Truth.

Truth can be approached on an intellectual level, emotional level, and intuitive level, and by directing all these three toward the Truth, Truth revels itself.

Truth is in the realm of feelingness, and cannot be expressed in words, but only alluded to by words.

Reason cannot get one to Truth, but can get one into the direction of Truth.

Intuition, knowingness, super-consciousness, reveals the Truth that is.

There's no Truth in the intellect. It's in the realm of feelingness. The intellect is used to guide the intellect to the feeling, which eventually takes over completely leaving no more intellect. Then one operates on purely intuitive feelings.

To know the Truth, begin with the Truth, that is, there is only an Infinite One. Then let your thinking follow from here.

Truth can be found by a process of eliminating wrong thoughts, which are thoughts of limitation. When all thoughts of limitation are eliminated, what remains is our natural, unlimited, Self.

Relative truth changes. Absolute Truth never changes. The Absolute Truth is the changeless Oneness, and Oneness in the only Truth.

Truth is perceived through realization.

When we realize Truth, we have it, are it, and can use it.

Absolute Truth cannot be spoken, because truth is Oneness and in Oneness there is no other to speak to. One merely alludes to Truth.

Truth and Reality are one and the same.

THE SELF (GOD)—WHAT IS IT?

The Self (God) is Infinite, Whole, Complete, Immutable, One, Perfect, Indivisible, Timeless, Eternal, Changeless, the only Reality.

> **MIND DETACHED FROM WORLD AND CENTERED ONLY ON SELF IS LIBERATION.**

The Self is our very beingness.

Nothing is more intimate than the Self (God).

The Self has no qualities, no abilities, no actions. It is unqualified and unlimited beingness.

We are now, we always have been, and we always will be the eternal, unlimited Self (God). All we need to do is to realize that by removing the ignorance of it, or by increasing our knowingness of it.

The easiest way to contact the Self (God) is through the feelingness in the heart of "I," or "I Am," with nothing more added. This feelingness is the Self, the Real—Inner Self. The moment we add anything at all, like "I am good or bad;" "I am poor or rich;" "I am great or small;" or "I and that;" we are imposing a limitation on the "I Am" and creating the ego.

There is no investigation possible into the Self (God). The Self, being only one, who is there to investigate it? Investigation can be only into the ego, the non-Self.

The Source of the ego is the Self. Find the Source and the ego disappears, leaving only the Self.

When we take one step toward the Self, It takes nine steps toward us.

What is it, by knowing which, everything becomes known? The Self (God).

What is joy? Joy is nothing but the Self. When desires are fulfilled, the mind is stilled. This allows the Self to shine forth and that is what we call joy.

When we let the inner self express, there are no problems.

Man, as man, cannot know God; by looking up to God, God is always separate from him. Only when he looks out from God can man know God.

One will never find God in the body, but one will find the body in God.

The higher the state of the body, the thinner the sheath hiding the Self.

God, generally, is the highest concept one has of oneself.

Stop having, stop doing, and just be your Self. At first this being your Self is momentary. As you keep trying, it remains more and more until it becomes permanent.

HOW TO HELP OTHERS

One who is not in some way helping others is injuring them. This "some way" is basically and generally in thought. Any thought other than one of good will or good wishes toward anyone, is injuring others and therefore injuring oneself.

The above is effected through the interconnection of all minds and by the act that the law of compensation, i.e., karma, is effected in the thought, whether the thought is carried through into action or not. Here are some additional thoughts on helping others.

———◦◦◦◦———

Your helping others is more by your attitude of how much you love them, than by your behavior.

———◦◦◦◦———

When you love you are very constructive whether you are in action or not. Just feel love and your thoughts will be those of love.

Thought is far more powerful than action. Thought is the basis of action. It is the initiator. It comes before it. It determines action.

———◦◦◦◦———

The degree of lack of recognition of woes of others is the degree of one's ego. The more one knows his Self, the more compassion and desire one has to help others.

The more you are capable of loving, the more you are helping the world.

All minds are interconnected, interactive and inter-react. The more an individual increases his love, the more everyone is helped.

Your thought force either helps or hurts the world's spiritual progress and is consequently hurting or helping yourself.

He who is not helping the world's upliftment is helping its degradation.

The greatest good is done by the person who best understands himself.

Everyone can be helped in every situation that involves more than one person, and no one has to be hurt when love determines.

When you let someone know you are doing something for them, they are obligated and return a "thank you." When they don't know and don't return, then the Infinite returns—overflowing!

—————

When I give and you give back, you stop me from receiving a blessing from the Infinite.

—————

It's helpful to you to help others, provided there's no ego motivation behind it and that it's done without attachment.

—————

A high being sitting in a cave somewhere all by himself is doing much good for the world by sending out powerful thoughts of love and peace.

—————

Charity is aiding and abetting the lie that God will take care of the sparrow but not man.

—————

Charity is saying, "You can't help yourselves."

Charity is good and necessary for one who is at that level of givingness and havingness.

The greatest thing we can do for others is to help them to help themselves.

Blessed is the giver because he is the happier—if he gives from his heart.

To the degree you straighten out yourself you may help others. Again I say, you're not going to help others any more than you help yourself. But try to help others because that will help you help yourself.

You don't need any special training to help others. You do it naturally, from your own state of beingness.

Everyone is a teacher teaching at his level. He does it unconsciously in his daily relationship with others.

The greatest givingness is not in things. The greatest givingness is your attitude of love.

Giving out money is like giving out snake protection (the snake and the rope concept). The greatest giving is giving the understanding that there is no snake to protect yourself from.

Have an attitude of givingness. It's not how much you give; it's your attitude. Some people give to hospitals etc. to get their nameplates on them, and that is the extent of their reward.

Whatever we do we should do with a desire to serve.

Serve with the feeling that it is not you but the God in you who serves.

The giver should say "Thank You" and the receiver should say, "You are welcome." (The giver is the more blessed).

The less ego we have the more we know the perfection of others. And it's to the degree that you know they're perfect that you support them in their being perfect.

A completely giving person always has whatever he wants.

We help mostly by raising our own state of being.

The higher you go the more you lift everyone.

When you're holding good thoughts, you're sending out good thoughts to everyone.

When you're helping others, where's your attention?

Selflessness is an excellent yardstick to measure the state of beingness of an individual.

Givingness is also a good yardstick. One's state of beingness is proportional to one's feeling of givingness, one's wanting to give.

Does a Master ask things from the devotees, the disciples? A Master is all-givingness.

Our feeling of givingness should be equal toward everyone. Giving to someone who likes you is ego motivated. A Master has equal-mindedness toward all.

Anyone who has spiritual pride is only giving out words, and the other one picks it up as words with no import or authority.

To help another one you have to equate him to you, i.e., not think you are spiritually higher.

When one understands, one sees everyone equally a master.

If everyone lived only for others that would right the world. It would make it a utopia!

When we live only for others, then we're at the top.

Any and every relationship should be for the purpose of helping the other one attain Realization, or for your being helped in attaining Realization.

Service to mankind will get full realization if you do it with no interest in the fruits thereof.

The Self is total Quietude. Quietness is necessary and one of the greatest ways to the Self.

The Self being One, the All, when one realizes this, one becomes, and identifies oneself as, every being, every atom, of the universe.

When one moves into or abides in the Self, one moves up and away from thoughts. The thoughts become submerged. Until one is established in the Self, the thoughts reemerge and take over. In moving away from thoughts, one can become the objective witness of the thoughts and not be influenced by them. When this objective witnessing is made permanent, one is in perfect, eternal, peace and joy. A fully realized individual does not identify with his thoughts and, therefore, they have no affect on him.

Self (God) is not subject to laws.

A knower of God has to wait only as long as he is not merged in God!

TEACHER OF TRUTH—HOW TO FIND ONE

How do I choose a real Teacher?

How do I know a Teacher is the right one to be followed?

What can a Teacher do for me? The qualifications of a Teacher of Truth are:

> *IF THERE IS ANYTHING IN THE WORLD WE LIKE OR DISLIKE, IT IS MASTER OVER YOU.*

- He is completely selfless and his every act is for others only.

- He has attained inner peace.

- He is equal-minded toward all.

- He must have experienced the knowledge he teaches.

- He is fearless.

- He gives freely of his knowledge with love.

- He has equal-mindedness towards all beings.

- He sees us as equal with himself.

- He expects nothing from anyone.

- He has no reactions.

- He is love that is all givingness.

- He loves all equally.

- He expects nothing from anyone.

- He is desireless.

- His every moment is oneness with God.

- He wants only God.

- He lives what he teaches.

- He sees no contradiction between human and divine.

Truth is, regardless of the Teacher. No one can make or unmake Truth. There is nothing new in Truth; it is eternal. A Teacher can direct one toward Truth, but each one must see it for himself and prove it. If the Teacher's or anyone's word is accepted, it is only hearsay. Anything the Teacher says should be accepted for checking. Only after proving it, does it become your knowledge.

A Teacher may be chosen intuitively. Intuition is tapping the source of omniscience within. It is a feeling. It is gotten with absolutely no thinking. Be there any thought with it, it is not intuition. When it comes, one knows that it is so and knows that he knows.

A Teacher lifts us high enabling us to perceive higher knowledge. He gives us the mental support that is helpful in getting the new realization.

A Teacher can lift one to his own level of understanding and no further.

One of the greatest things a Teacher can do for us is to get us to see our ego. We have blinded ourselves to our ego making it most difficult to let go of it.

A Teacher has a quieting effect on our minds.

A Teacher keeps one in the consciousness of the right direction.

A Teacher makes the way easier.

A Teacher is more helpful than scriptures and books.

THE EGO—WHAT IS IT?

Ego is the sense of individuality as opposed to the One.

The start of the ego is the sense of "I am separate." It then creates thoughts, (called mind) of limitation like "I am body," or "I am body limited," through which thoughts one loses sight of the fact that one is Infinite.

> IF I GIVE YOU SOMETHING BECAUSE I WANT YOU TO LIKE ME, THAT IS NOT LOVE; THAT IS TRYING TO BOLSTER MY EGO.

Ego comes from the subconscious knowledge of the terrific Being that we really are, trying to express itself through a very limited thing called the personality.

The I-thought, the thought that "I am a separate individual," is the source of the ego in all its forms—physical, astral, and causal. Every day one goes through the physical, astral, and causal realms in waking, dreaming and dreamless sleep, respectively. Eliminate the ego and all three states are eliminated.

Until we become fully free, we put up a false front, a façade, to others for the purpose of winning the acceptance and approval of the others. We behave in accordance with what we think the other one wants rather than by expressing our own real feelings.

We thereby develop a distorted pattern of behavior that becomes habitual, automatic, and subconscious. This pattern necessitates unhappiness, as we become incapable of expressing our own true feelings.

The subconscious automatic behavior, by its very nature, blinds us to ourselves, others, and the world. To be happy, it is necessary to see things as they really are.

This may be done by (1) reevaluating the situation by seeing its present time reality; (2) digging into the subconscious in order to make it conscious so that we may change it; (3) perceiving our real Self.

The façade is the ego. It is motivated by our seeking love. The only reward is frustration, as it is only by loving that one finds love.

Seek the Source of the ego and it disappears.

The greater the misery, the greater the ego.

Misery can be removed by seeing its cause as being the ego seeking love. Only by loving can one be happy.

In these days of atom smashing, the only safety is ego smashing! Ego smashing is one of the fastest ways toward the Goal and the only safety.

We create an ego and then try to escape from it from that moment on.

When the ego disappears, only God remains.

The God-part of us is there all the time—just covered over by the ego.

Who is doing the striving? The ego. Let go, and let God.

All the power and grace of God is at every moment trying to come through to us. All we need to do is allow it by setting the ego aside, scorching it by ignoring it. An unrecognized vision soon leaves.

THE MIND—WHAT IS IT?

Mind is consciousness that has assumed limitation. We are naturally unlimited until we assume a mind. Then the evolution begins of progressively limiting ourselves until we can no longer bear it.

> DISCOVER WHO THE SUFFERER IS AND ON DISCOVERING THIS YOU FIND ALL JOY.

When life becomes altogether unbearable, we then start the devolution. We reverse the process by letting go of thoughts more and more until the complete peace and total freedom from thought is reestablished.

One makes life easier by recognizing the laws of nature, which are only the laws of cause and effect. When one discovers that mind or thinking is the cause, and what happens in the world is effect, he then consciously controls his circumstances and environment.

The mind is nothing but the sum-total of all thoughts and all thoughts are concepts of limitation.

That which we think—we create. That which we hold in mind—we sustain. That which we let go of in mind—we dissolve.

When we quiet the mind by letting go of thoughts of limitation, we see this infinite being that we are.

Stay on the positive side. Do not be "against" (anti) anything, but be "for" its opposite. "Being against" is holding in mind that which you do not want and thereby sustaining it.

Every thought is causative.

That which your mind is on, you become!

Whatever happens to us originates in the mind.

Think only what you want that that is all that you will get.

It is impossible to get rid of a problem, because ridding oneself is holding it in mind and thereby sustaining it!

The more the thought taking, the greater the problem. The less the thought taking, the more obvious the Perfection.

Mind is an instrument used by the ego to create and then reflect back the physical universe.

The world is an out-projecting of the mind. When we realize this, we can change the projected picture.

Mind is intelligent; body is insentient matter.

Body is the materialization of mind.

The body is an exact copy of the mind.

The moment the mind is right, the body is right.

Disease of the body is dis-ease of the mind.

Suffering is in mind. When the body hurts, it is felt in the mind.

Thinking is rationalizing, usually our emotions and desires, and has its source in the ego. Thinking can be used to make life easier for the ego by causing the world to ease its pull on our attention. Then our attention can be better directed to the Self (God).

Correct thinking is thinking that leads us to good conditions of health and supply, then to mental traits of love and peace, and finally to Oneness, where, there being no other, thought is impossible and all is in harmony.

Taking it from the top, the most correct thinking is "no thoughts." Truth is in the realm of knowingness. It is when all thoughts are stilled that we remove the blanket covering the omniscience that we all have now.

Pure Mind is mind with no thoughts. It is knowingness.

Pure Mind allows the omnipresent omniscience to flow through us.

Real knowledge lies just behind thought which is relative knowledge.

The mind will never know God because the mind is a thing of limitation.

The finite can never know the Infinite.

The only thing which blinds us from the Self is mind activity.

Mind (1) gives rise to thoughts of desire (2) that lead to attachments and aversions (3) causing bondage. Eliminate any one in this chain and be free!

Habit makes us believe that it is difficult to stop thinking. If the error is discovered by realizing one's inner state of all-knowingness, one would not foolishly and unnecessarily burden oneself with the effort of thinking.

Habits of thought are latent tendencies and are the greatest enemy to realization. They are most stubborn and adamant. However, they must be let go of if one wants to realize the Self.

Intellectual knowing is merely like a tape recording; real knowing is understanding, and can be tested by the fruits.

Our intellectual knowledge is used by the ego as a substitute for real knowledge.

The mind is a composite of several functions: sensing, recording, memory, and ability to discriminate. Discrimination is the highest function.

Discriminate Truth from untruth, the Real from the unreal—and be free!

The mind never forgets—it just doesn't recall at the moment.

Mind is about 90% subconscious. The 10% must be used to make it all conscious.

Every mind is a transmitting and a receiving station, receiving in its own wavelength. Keep it high!

Mental efficiency is in the art of concentration.

The mind is like an electric light bulb radiating in all directions. When it is focused, it becomes like a powerful beam. A mind focused on itself will crack its secrets and reveal Truth.

A concentrated mind is one that can keep its attention on one thing at a time without other thoughts coming in.

A concentrated mind is the secret of success in the realization of Truth.

A concentrated mind is also the secret of success in the world. All successful people in the world have the ability to concentrate their minds.

Real solitude can be had only in the mind; not in location. Solitude is obtained through practice of non-attachment. A man in the city might be free of thought and alone in peace, while a hermit in the country might be plagued with the company of many miserable thoughts.

Thoughts of happiness give relative happiness. The highest and absolute happiness is beyond thoughts.

LESTER ON DEMONSTRATION

Whether we are aware of it or not, everyone is controlling matter all the time. Whether one wants to be a demonstrator or not, he is. It is impossible to not be a creator all the time. Everyone is creating every day. We're not aware of it because we just don't look at it. Every thought, every single thought materializes in the physical world. It's impossible to have a thought that will not materialize, except that we reverse it. If we say the opposite right after we have a thought of equal strength, we just neutralize it. But any thought not reversed or neutralized will materialize in the future, if not immediately. So this thing of demonstration that we're all trying so hard to do we're doing all the time, unaware of the fact that we are doing it. All we need to do is to consciously direct it, and that we call demonstration.

Everything that everyone has in life is a demonstration. It could not come into your experience had you not had a thought of it sometime prior. If you want to know what your sum total thinkingness is, it's exactly determined by what's around you, what you have. That is your demonstration. If you like it you may hold it—if you don't, start changing your thinking, concentrate it in the direction that you really want, until those thoughts become predominant, and whatever those thoughts are will materialize in the world. And when you begin to demonstrate consciously—small things—you may then realize that the only reason why they're small is because you don't dare to think big. But the exact same rule of principle applies to demonstrating a penny that applies to demonstrating a billion dollars. The mind sets the size. Anyone who can demonstrate a dollar can demonstrate a million dollars. Become aware of the way you're demonstrating the one dollar bill and just put six zeroes after it next time. Take on the consciousness of the million, rather than the one dollar bill.

This relates to what I have been saying that there's no difference between the spiritual and the material when you see it, the material being just an out-projecting of our minds into what we call the universe and the world, and many bodies. And when we see that it is just an out-projecting of our mind, it's just a picture out there that we have created, we can very easily change it. Instantly. So to repeat: Everyone is demonstrating, creating, every moment that he or she is thinking. You have no choice. You are a creator, so long as you have a mind and think. To get beyond creation, we must go beyond the mind, and just behind the mind is the realm of all Knowingness, where there's no need for creation. There's a higher state than creation: It's a state of is-ness, of being-ness, sometimes called Awareness, Beingness, Consciousness. That's just behind the mind. That's beyond creation. The mind finds it very difficult to imagine what it's like beyond creation, because the mind is involved primarily in creation, in creating. It's the creating instrument of the universe and everything that happens in the world, in the universe. So if you take this thing called mind, which is only a creator, and try to imagine what it is like beyond creation, it's impossible. The mind will never know peace (quiet) because you have to go just above the mind to know peace (quiet) to know the Infinite Being that we are, to know what it's like beyond creation. The final state is beyond creation. The ultimate State is the changeless state. In creation, everything is constantly changing, therefore in creation the Ultimate Truth is not there. So to demonstrate what one wants, one needs to become aware of the fact that all we need to do is think only of the things we want, and that is all that we would get, if we would do just that. Only think of the things you want, and that's what you'll be getting all the time, because the mind is only creative. Nice and easy, isn't it? Also, take credit for all the things you create that you don't like—just say, "Oh, look what I did"—because when you become aware that you've created things you don't like, you're still in a position of creator, and if you don't like it, all you have to do is turn it upside down and you'll like it.

THE WORLD

All behavior, **every act in this world**, is based on the desire for love. This desire causes us to seek for approval, acceptance, attention, power, fame, and fortune.

> THE HIGHEST ENJOYMENT IN THE WORLD IS A MERE PITTANCE COMPARED TO YOUR NATURAL INHERENT STATE OF YOU.

Unfortunately, however, love cannot be gotten this way, and we become frustrated and unhappy. Only by loving can we find love and be happy.

The world has moments of pleasure with far more pain in between.

Man was never intended to be a victim of circumstances. He is the controller of them, but has lost awareness of this fact. When he regains his awareness of it, he again becomes the master of circumstances, and consciously controls his environment.

The world beats you until you know your self.

Matter, energy, space, and time are in mind. When man realizes this, he has mental control over them and controls them at his will.

Use the world to transcend the world. Look at your attachments and aversions to it and drop them.

There is not intelligence in matter. The world is nothing but matter. The intelligence that is in man, and it determines this world. However, man is unconsciously determining the world. When he wakes up to this, he gains conscious control.

There is no world without the one who sees it.

Perceiving the Reality one gains dominion.

Only a realized non-attached being can enjoy things in the world without creating boundaries and miseries.

Creation is a mental projection. The Reality is just behind it!

The world does not disappear on seeing the Reality; the wrong concept of it does!

The world is a school in which there is only limitation. The lessons on limitations teach us how to surmount them until we are limitless.

Life in the world necessitates misery, as it is in the realm of limitation. Be in the world, but not of it!

When one cannot bear being alone with his thoughts, he seeks entertainment. Entertainment is escaping, running away from one's thoughts. Happiness needs no entertainment. Be happy by loving. The more one loves, the less one needs entertainment.

Socializing is looking for love in the wrong place. It's looking for love and acceptance from people. And what we really want is the love of God. Love of God is found only by going within quietness. It is loving, and not looking for love.

Pleasures gained in the world are momentary. Any joy gained through understanding the Truth or the Reality is eternally ours.

You want to help the world? Help yourself. Only then may you do so. You cannot show others unless you know yourself.

That which we give out to the world we receive in return— is the law of compensation (karma). Many know this but few realize that karma is created in the thought rather than the act.

If we want good and happy lives it is necessary to think good and happy thoughts only.

If one gossips about others, one does not hurt the other one, but hurts himself in accord with the law of compensation. Gossip is a form of hatred because it tears down the other.

When one judges, the ego is playing God.

Anything we deem right or wrong is judging.

Any thinking that is "anti" (against) is judgment.

Harmlessness and mutuality always direct one into correct behavior.

There's no right or wrong, good or bad. There's only experiencing for the purpose of learning the Reality.

There's nothing wrong with the world when you see it alright.

The only way out of the world is through the world by seeing every atom of it as your Self.

Socializing and entertainment are wasting time because what we are really looking for (constant and unlimited joy) is not there.

Time used in releasing meditation and selfless service is the most useful time. It leads to joy infinite.

If each moment wasted in pursuit of the non-Self utilized in pursuit of the Self, realization will soon follow.

Work or action need not be an obstruction to Self-Realization. The search for your Self can always go on. One should work or act with non-attachment, and take the attitude that he is not the doer. Just be the witness. Then releasing meditation can go on, and through practice, it becomes constant.

A night dream best explains this world. All suffering in a nightmare is real to us while we are dreaming. The entire creation of the world, its characters, and our part in it—all of these, while we are dreaming, seem real. It is only when we awaken that we become aware that it never was, and that is all subjective. Likewise, when we awaken from this world, we say that it never was, and that it is subjective. Then we see the Reality, the singular substance of the world which is just behind it.

In the most limited state called wakefulness, one must see that he is limitless. Awakening from this wakeful state awakens one to his unlimited Self.

SEX AND MARRIAGE

Realization is not determined by one's being single or married, but by the realization of who he is. A married man may realize the Self by learning to concentrate his mind. A concentrated mind will do it.

> **THE FIRST PLACE TO PRACTICE LOVE IS IN THE HOME WITH FAMILY. WE SHOULD TRY TO LOVE OUR FAMILY MORE AND MORE BY ALLOWING THEM THEIR RIGHT TO BE THE WAY THEY ARE.**

Real love should be the basis of marriage. Real love has no element of needing the other one, or possessing the other one. Real love wants only to make the other one happy.

Marriage should be used to aid one's growth by developing love more and more—until it is complete.

If you are a parent, the greatest help you can give your child is to help yourself to a higher state of loving. Then you automatically do what is best for the child. Following rules from books will not be very effective.

See your spouse and children as children of God. Never say, "They are mine," as they are God's.

Increase your selfless love for them until it is Divine Love.

The greatest happiness we can give to a mate comes from helping him or her to more understanding of Truth.

Don't marry because you feel you need, or you must possess, the other one. This is not love and will have its consequent unhappiness.

The happiest marriage is one in which each partner lives only for the other's happiness. This is a love marriage and helps one toward the goal.

Marriage is too frequently only a sexual union. One marries a member of the opposite sex and sex is freely pursued. Marriage should be a love union.

Man is confused on sex. Sex is a physical union of male and female, the purpose of which is procreation. The greatest attachments man has are to sex. Man ties in two other things with sex, one mental and one spiritual. The mental aspect is the desire for ego approval. The spiritual aspect is love.

Man has gone so far astray from the normal that he can no longer get any standards as to what is correct, normal sex. He might realign himself by looking at the animals to learn the purpose and function of sex. If he does, he will see it—a physical act of procreation.

But man is higher than the animal and is gifted with a mind much further developed than the animal. Animals think only deductively while man thinks not only deductively but also inductively. The latter gives him the ingenuity to do all that he does that is greater than the animal. This inductive thinking allows man to be self-conscious. Man knows he is man. Animals know only the ways and means of procuring and satisfying the needs for preservation. Only man looks into himself and seeks, thereby advancing himself.

The mental aspect of sex is the seeking for ego approval. Man looks for a partner that can give it to him, and when he finds one that can give him ego approval constantly, he says he is madly in love, and wants this one as a constant mate. So long as he is getting this approval, direct or implied, he says he is in love and happy. However, and this is a big however, this happiness, although it may be the greatest he has yet experienced, is of necessity at the same time mixed with a certain amount of painful anxiety lest this happiness be not had in the time ahead. The pleasure obtained through one's mate creates a hunger for more of it, and at the same time a fear that it could be lost, both of which are painful. This mixture of pain and pleasure necessarily prevents full enjoyment.

What is constant and totally satisfying is the love aspect. Only when man really loves his partner in the full meaning of love as defined in the preceding chapter on love, will he be joyous and happy every moment of his life.

It is the love aspect of sex that man is really and unconsciously seeking. Unfortunately, he has lost sight of this and when he sees it, and regains it, he will be continuously happy.

Sex in moderation is better than indulgence. Indulgence keeps one bogged down and blinded.

Sex, of body passion, hinders growth by imprisoning one into the body cage. Sex, when it rises to the passion of the spirit, is channeled into expansion of love and liberation.

Sex is a trap. Sex leads to birth. If there is birth, there must be death. Thus man goes from death to death. (Seek your immortality.)

The desire for sex is basically the desire for love and when it is satisfied in sex, the drive to attain the real Love is weakened.

The power of the sex drive may be directed into channels of love that will give a thousand times more joy than the greatest joy that sex can give.

Attain to the joy that is so much greater than that which sex gives, so that in order to have sex, we have to give up a greater joy for a lesser pleasure.

We should try to attain to the understanding of Truth to the point where we have no desire for sex or human affection, but instead have a constant joy greater than that which sex or human affection can give.

Joy is not in things or people. The joy attributed to them comes only from the Self shining forth when thoughts are stilled. The thoughts are stilled by the satisfying of the desire.

Sex deludes us in that it brings us closest to the Self (God). By satisfying the greatest desire, the greatest number of thoughts, conscious and subconscious, are stilled. When the thoughts are stilled, your Self shines forth and that is the wonderful feeling of peace and satisfaction that you feel. This wonderful feeling should be gotten directly and made constant.

DESIRE—WHAT IS IT?

Thought and desire are the same.

> **DESIRE IS THE MOTHER OF ALL MOTION, THE DISTURBER OF ALL PEACE.**

We should strive to attain to the desirelessness state. As long as we have desire, we lack, and are trapped in the world of limitation. Desire is the great enemy of constant joy.

A desire is a disturbance of one's natural, inherent peace and joy.

Any desire, other than desiring knowledge of the Self (God), pushes one in the opposite direction of happiness, into limitation and misery. The more desire one has for things, the more unhappiness one has.

Any time you have any problem there's desire behind it.

Desire and chain are the same. Every time one gratifies one's desire, one creates a bondage as he wants it again and again.

Desire is the enemy of happiness and the source of misery.

Enjoying with attachment is enjoying with pain and longing, a hunger. Enjoying without attachment is enjoying freely and creating no bondage.

Every time one tries to satisfy a desire, he creates a [don't understand the word] intensity of that desire.

Letting go of attachments is an excellent method of growth.

Desire is seeking the joy of being our Self through objects and people.

Everything we own, owns us.

The only possibility of satiety is to remain in your Self.

The way to infinite joy is through the elimination of desire—no attachments, no aversions.

The more we turn desire off, the weaker it becomes.

When your Self is known, you are fully satisfied and have everything.

It is not necessary to understand the negative. It is far better to be the positive.

One should have only one desire—the desire for complete liberation.

Desire is an admission of lack.

Try to attain the state of dispassion—no attachments, no aversions.

EMOTION—WHAT IS IT?

Emotions are strong feelings. They result from thwarted will. They are really the feelings of the absence of

> **EMOTION SICKNESS IS CATCHING.**

love, with a desire to eliminate this absence.

Examine human emotion and you will always find elements of thwarted will or desire. Human love desires to possess the one loved. Whatever one desires to possess, one must feel one does not have. This is the element that makes human love incapable of constant happiness.

Emotions excite and perturb. The opposite is calmness, quietness, peace. Real love, being calm and peaceful, is not an emotion.

Emotion is the opposite of peace.

Emotion is a thing of the ego.

Emotion is ego in motion.

Emotion blinds us and hinders perception and efficiency of thought.

To act with complete freedom, there must be no emotion. We are blinded to what is really going on to the degree of our emotion.

A suppressed emotion is one that we have pushed down into the subconscious part of the mind and have become aware of it.

Any suppressed emotion will forever try to spend itself until it is spent.

Suppressed emotions and thoughts develop compulsions and inhibitions, setting habits of wrong behavior.

Most behavior is distorted and rooted in suppressed emotions and thoughts.

Never suppress feelings. You don't have to satisfy them, but don't suppress them. Just know that they are there, and let go of them.

A desire in the past is a subconscious desire in the present.

A desire today becomes a subconscious desire in the future.

A reaction is an automatic response determined by a past behavior.

A reaction is a behavior based on a past incident in which one felt pain, mental or physical. When something happens in the present that unconsciously reminds one of the past incident, one automatically acts as though the past incident were present now with its prospective pain, and unconsciously tries to avoid that pain. This caused the behavior in the present to be determined by conditions in the past, and it is not in accord with the present situation. This results in very inefficient behavior that cannot bring satisfaction. It makes one unhappy for two reasons, one being the unconscious reminder of pain, and the other, the frustration of not being able to achieve the desired result of the present act.

Reactive behavior is not free behavior.

Free behavior is that which is determined by a consideration of the circumstances at the moment and not conditioned by the circumstances of some previous or past incident.

To the degree that we react, we blind ourselves to what is out there. We then see the world through our own colored glasses.

Reactive behavior should be approached as an opportunity for growth. Each time we reevaluate a reactive behavior pattern and let go of it, we become freer.

By tracing all reactions to their source, we eliminate reactions.

Eliminate all reactive behavior and be free!

PLEASURE/PAIN—WHAT IS IT?

Pleasure is the feeling we have when that which is happening is liked.

Pain, similarly, is the feeling we have when that which is happening is not liked.

> **THE ONLY WAY OUT OF ALL DIFFICULTIES IS TO KNOW THAT YOU ARE NOT THE BODY.**

Pleasure results from the stilling of thoughts by satisfying them, thus allowing our real Self to shine forth a bit more.

Pain results from more thoughts being created. Thoughts obscure the Self.

It is the mind which tells us that something is pleasurable or painful. Does the body tell us it is hurting?

To some, pleasure is the avoidance of pain. This is a negative approach and allows little of the infinite joy that is available.

Pain acknowledges limitation.

Pain becomes a habit.

Pain is a prod to push us in the right direction.

The right direction is to know that we are masters over body and mind.

The more we look in the right direction, the more we find that which is right and true, and the less the pain.

There is more pain from holding on to the thought of pain than there is in the situation itself. If you let the world strike you, it will do so less cruelly than your own imagination.

Pain in the body is the sense of heightened awareness at a point. When a part of the body is being damaged, a mental alarm is turned on, called pain. If the mind answers the alarm fully, the pain turns off immediately, and the body mechanics go to work at that point and rapidly repair it. Because of past unpleasant experiences, we have developed a fear of pain, and mentally try to flee from it, to escape it. This is not fully answering the alarm; it causes the pain to linger, and the body repair mechanics to slow down. If one knows this, he can eliminate pain and effect a rapid healing of the body. It not being easy to understand what "feeling the pain" means, try increasing the pain. This mentally places one in the pain and makes one feel it. On really feeling the pain it will immediately disappear and the body will rapidly heal.

Mental pain likewise can be eliminated by recognizing it and facing it. A mental problem, when faced fully and squarely, will resolve. Because of its unpleasantness, one tries to flee from it and escape it. This holds it in mind rather than resolves it, and thereby holds onto the pain.

Looking for pleasure is part of the unconscious drive toward the infinite joy that is inherently yours.

HEALTH AND SUPPLY—HOW TO GET IT

It is the same principle that heals a sick body or a sick pocketbook.

Sickness and poverty are both lack, and lack is the acceptance of concepts that are limited.

> **DISCOVER WHO THE SUFFERER IS AND ON DISCOVERING THIS YOU FIND ALL.**

The concept of lack is only in our consciousness. One must let go of it and in its place have concepts of abundance, affluence, and well being.

When one learns, by actually experiencing it that mind is only creative, he then holds in mind only the things he wants and never takes thought for the things he does not want.

Our concepts are the sum total of our thinking and most of them are now subconscious. We must, with effort, hold the right concepts until they become more powerful than the subconscious wrong concepts. Then they become the habit and take the place of the wrong concepts. When the subconscious mind is so conditioned life becomes beautiful and happy.

Man's behavior today is about 90% determined by his subconscious thinking. He is acting automatically and is determined by his past, and now subconscious, ideas and concepts. That is why he finds it so difficult to make correct thinking effective. It is necessary to persevere with correct thinking until it becomes the habit by overriding the subconscious habit.

It is possible to eliminate years of accumulated wrong thinking in one single thought if that one thought be powerful enough, that is, effected with tremendous will.

Our supply and health are determined by our consciousness of supply and health.

A mental picturing of that which we want, with the complete acceptance and the conviction that it is ours now, will bring it quickly. See it in its 'isness.'

Never think of things as coming in the future, as the mind will keep it in the future. See it, feel it, taste it, possess it as yours now. Do not see it in its 'will-be-ness.'

Picture things in the fullness of detail.

Think of what you want, never the money to obtain it. Conditioning it with money is putting a limitation in the way.

Work in secrecy. Telling one what you want weakens the drive. After obtaining it, you may tell.

Repetition is not desirable in that it means we did not accept it fully the time before. However, if necessary, repeat the visualization.

A full conviction that we have everything that we need as we need it will do just that.

Supply is infinite. Never compete.

No matter how sick the body, it may be made perfect.

If we desire something, it is an admission of lack. When we realize the God-Being that we are, we feel that everything is ours. When this realization is obtained, the thought of something brings it to us.

When we know that we have everything and therefore need nothing, then everything comes to us for the mere effortless thought of it.

Never connect your supply with your vocation. Let God be your supplier. Then it matters not what you do as your supply is guaranteed.

Effectiveness power depends on what you know of the principle.

To effect anything, complete passivity is the quickest way. Let go and let God. It's a doingness on the mental plane, a knowingness on the spiritual plane that everything is ours.

The key to prosperity is in the spirit of giving. When we know that freely it is given, then freely we give, and the more do we receive.

If one can heal oneself spiritually one should do it because it is instantaneous. If one cannot do it spiritually, then one should do it mentally as mental healing is from rapid to instantaneous. If one cannot do it mentally, then one should do it physically seeing a doctor.

Spiritual healing is knowing that the body is perfect. Mental healing is effecting a perfect body by visualizing the body as perfect.

Rather than receive a healing of body or pocket book it is better to receive the understanding of healing. Then one may be always free from all lack.

The fastest and surest way to health and prosperity is by understanding Truth.

SPIRITUAL GROWTH—WHAT IS IT?

When one takes the path and begins to grow, all latent tendencies, strong and weak, are intensified and brought forth for

> **THIS ENTIRE PATH IS A DO-IT-YOURSELF PATH.**

mastering. Rather than lose the self-initiated trial between your will to grow and the karmic enemies that would dethrone you, it is necessary that you should be willing to lose everything in order to gain the goal. This must be so.

All life experiences are wasted, and one only postpones his reinstating of infinite joy , if he does not use the experiences of life to learn from. Every single unpleasantness has a lesson of joy in it.

When one chooses to grow, his life becomes a paradox to those of the world. Any attempt to justify it makes it appear the more hopelessly contradictory. In calmness and quietness is your strength. Silently let your growth so shine that the quietness loudly proclaims to them the greatness of your way.

Growth is evolution in reverse, that is, the undoing of the limitations we have learned over the centuries, and takes time and continual doing.

Growth is becoming free. As we grow, we must become freer and freer from behavior conditioned by compulsions and inhibitions learned in early training. Likewise, we must free ourselves from behavior based on traditions.

Freedom is to do, or not to do, as we choose.

To be happy, one must be good by choice. Being good because one feels he must be, should be, or is compelled to be good, does not bring happiness as this is not a free choice.

A greater obstacle is overcome by a greater truth.

Opposition is a very healthy thing. It provokes and firms growth.

The more the growth, the simpler everything is.

Use every down as an up.

Growth is the eliminating of the ego and the realizing of your Self.

When the ego is zero, God is all.

One must raise oneself up to the level of spiritual knowledge to perceive it. It does not come down to the level where it is not.

Rate of growth is directly proportional to the intensity of the desire for it.

Only by realizing Truth does one know Truth.

A realization is recognition of some Truth within.

It is through realizations that we grow.

When we realize, we know, and we know that we know.

A realization is like a bright light turning on in the mind revealing something apparently new. The fact is that it has always been there and we are re-remembering it.

Realization is revelation.

The greatest realization is that we have always been fully realized beings; that all we need do is remove the ignorance of this fact.

Releasing is the way to realization.

RELEASING

Releasing is directing your thoughts inwardly with the desire to find and know your Self (God).

> **LET GO OF YOUR EGO—AND BE YOUR SELF!**

Correct meditation is holding the thought on Self (God) to the exclusion of all other thoughts.

Releasing stills the thoughts of the world and its tumult and allows one to see his Self.

Concentration, holding one thought to the exclusion of other thoughts, is the key to successful meditation.

Releasing is not becoming passive. Don't try to go blank as anything can come in.

The best question to think on is, "Who am I?"

Any question fed into the mind will bring an answer if we await it. However, we frequently reject the answer the moment it comes.

Releasing ultimately leads to complete quietude of mind with its blissful peace.

Releasing is daily separation of man from the world, only to unite him more closely and more intimately with it, by becoming one with it.

Releasing is a supplication to the Self to enter and abide; to show us the glory of the Self, so that we will want only it, rather than the ego.

PRACTICAL METHODS
THAT MAY BE USED DAILY

Correct Behavior
There are only two laws that need be known to cover all correct behavior.

> **PERSEVERANCE IS NECESSARY.**

1. One should have a feeling of harmlessness toward all beings.

2. That which is mutual is correct.

By following only these two rules one will be guided correctly in all situations, and will be aided in one's growth.

Square all with love.

Accept full responsibility for whatever happens to you. By taking full responsibility and seeking the cause in your thinking, you will find the initiating cause and eliminate it.

Discriminate between the Real, that which is changeless, and the unreal, that which changes.

Attain to the desirelessness state.

Attain to the place where no one and no thing can disturb you.

Be a witness, unaffected; assuming the place where you should be.

Get to the point where you see the perfection where the seeming imperfection seems to be.

See your Self in everyone and everything.

Develop a constant feeling of gratitude toward God and everyone. This makes one always joyous.

Grant the other one the other one's beingness.

Get quiet.

Concentrate your mind.

Develop a constant consciousness of your path and goal.

Keep Holy company. Seek those who are seeking Truth. Read only that which is directing and aiding your growth.

Daily, let go of the ego.

Take no thought for the ego—take thought only for your Self.

Let the ego go its way and know that it is not the real you, your Self. Just keep knowing that you are not it. Eventually, it not being recognized, it will vanish!

Review your behavior of the day, at the end of each day, as a means of rapid growth. Square all with love, reviewing the behavior in the light of love, and take full responsibility for whatever happened.

Examination of behavior, in the light of love, with those whom one feels closest to, is very revealing and helpful to one's growth.

Practice loving those who oppose you. Be sure you are not suppressing your opposition. If there is opposition or hate, recognize it with the attitude that this, too, shall pass.

Introspection brings up the subconscious and makes it conscious, allowing us to change it.

Reactions can be used as opportunities for growth by seeking their source and thereby eliminating them.

Accentuate the positive, eliminate the negative and don't have anything to do with Mr.-in-between.

It is better to act wrongly than to not act. No action is paralyzing. By wrong action one will learn right action.

Submit either to God within, your Inner Self, or God without, the Teacher, and unload your burdens.

We are here and now fully a Realized Being telling ourselves that we are not, by saying, "I need this," "I need that," "I am limited by this," "I am limited by that." All we need to do is to stop feeling that we are limited and start being the unlimited being that we really are.

WAYS OF GETTING OUT OF A BLUE MOOD INTO A HAPPY MOOD

FILL YOURSELF TO THE FULL WITH SELFLESS LOVE.

Square all with love.

Be cause and not effect.

Ex-press and be not im-pressed.

Think what you want and stop thinking of what you do not want.

Face it.

Pick an agreement with the other one.

Resist nothing.

Accept everything. (Including yourself and your thoughts.)

Know that the help is always there, because God never forsakes.

DIFFERENT PATHS—HOW TO GET THERE

> *YOU HAVE TO UNWANT THE WORLD AND*
> *WANT YOUR SELF.*

There are five major paths to Self Realization to suit the various natures and inclinations of man. They are:

- Using the release technique by using Self-Inquiry and looking within and asking the question, "Who am I?"

- Right Understanding through use of one's intellect and wisdom.

- Mind Control through breath control.

- Devotion through love of, and surrender to, God.

- Action through selfless service to humanity.

- The paths all end up answering the question "Who am I?"

THOUGHTS

That which you are seeking is seeking you more so.

This is the study of the causes and purposes of life and takes as its premise that man is potentially an unlimited being—that whatever he is capable of thinking, he is capable of

> *USE THE WORLD TO TRANSCEND THE WORLD. LOOK AT YOUR ATTACHMENTS AND AVERSIONS TO IT AND DROP THEM.*

doing. The evolutionary purpose in life is to find more and more this limitless being that man is. The practicality of the study is that as man lets go of his limitations, he becomes a freer, healthier, and happier being.

We have infinite power within us, and no thing or no one can hurt us until we give them the power to.

No one can be helped by a higher being unless desirous of it and ready for it. Higher teachers present their teaching and one may pick it up or not, as one chooses. The relationship of Teacher and pupil is one of a mutuality.

Earth is a classroom to which we come to learn the eternal Truths.

A Consciousness of Truth meets no resistance.

All experiences contain a lesson. If the lesson is difficult, the same difficulty keeps repeating itself until resolved in the light of Truth.

Heaven and hell are right where we are and are created by our thinking. When we know this, we make it only heaven.

Liberation is acquired through understanding alone! Right action does not free, but is an aid to freedom.

Confirmation from one who has dipped into the Self is very helpful. It assures you that you are right even though all the others may think you are wrong.

As we grow we acquire new ways of thought and new friends in place of the old. Eventually we see all as our friends.

The higher the joy, the higher you may go! Joy is unlimited!

One must stand out and be separate, and never let go of Principle. If one does, he steps down.

One with God is a majority.

"One with God" is an absolute safety.

The worldly limited concepts do not let go easily. They are deeply ingrained over many millenniums, and fight (via the ego) for survival.

How long does it take for Omniscience and Omnipotence to know that It is?!

Man, in trying to regain his limitlessness, tried to conquer matter, energy, space, and time through science and external machines. When he recognizes his ability to do this directly there results clairvoyance, clairaudience, telepathy, telekinetic, teleportation, etc.

We do not have to react to disagreeable words. Words are sounds with but tiny bits of energy impinging on our eardrums. Let this infinitesimal energy affect you not.

No one's word can affect us unless we accept that it can.

If you want someone to do something and he doesn't, it's up to you to feel hurt. The other person doesn't hurt you— you do!

Whose feelings are you feeling when you feel hurt? If they are yours you are doing it. If you are doing it, you can not do it.

Good intentions are no substitute for the doing of the thing.

Blame is a substitute for correcting one's behavior. Blame is a shame.

What you do is not nearly as important as the attitude with which you do it.

It's impossible to be happy when one is dependent on others.

We're happy when we are ex-pressing, but we're miserable when we're being im-pressed.

Your answer should be "yes" or "no," but never "maybe." It's better to take wrong action than to take no action. By wrong action one learns right action. Maybe becomes paralyzing to a human being.

We should be cause and not effect.

He that excuses, accuses himself.

To be free is to have a choice to do or not to do a thing. Complete freedom would allow us to walk down a main street nude. However, to do this would be foolish, as it would result in arrest and other trouble. What is required for freedom is the ability to do it, but not the doing of it.

Living the way others live is non-freedom.

Do not try to correct a problem. Behold the real Perfection and this frees you of an assumed imperfection.

God is All and God is Perfect, and when one sees that, one can see only the Perfection where the seeming imperfections seem to be.

There can be only perfection for one if that is his only thinking.

There's nothing out there but your consciousness.

When we see imperfection without, we should look within.

Only that which is within can be seen without.

You don't like the world out there? Change yourself.

Thinking is cause, what happens is effect.

See no evil, hear no evil, think no evil, and there will be no evil for you.

There is never any other time but the present moment, the past is always in the past, and the future is always in the future.

Let go of past life and future life. Know the truth of the present and you will know everything.

Time is a series of present moments.

Time is a mental concept.

All minds are interconnected. Otherwise they could not understand each other.

Anytime one is thinking in misery, one is moving downward and in the wrong direction. Likewise, when one is thinking in joy, one is happy and is moving upward and in the right direction. When the movement upward is greater than the movement downward, the resultant progress is upward.

Don't probe darkness to understand light.

Don't dwell on sickness to be healthy.

Don't indulge in thoughts of lack to have supply.

Don't dwell in misery to understand happiness.

Everything we own has a mouth and must be fed.

Everything we own owns us.

God, like the sun, shines equally on all. It is not the fault of the sun if the plant is weak.

God never forsakes,- man does!

Grace is always constant and full. We receive it according to the degree of our receptivity.

Transfer your allegiance from the creation to the Creator.

Surrender is a radical reliance.

Devotion is willing the ego into subsidence.

Humility of the ego is wonderful. When the ego gets small, the God-part gets bigger. But don't think that you are presumptuous when you say "I Am That I Am," because that is your inherent nature.

The less the ego, the quieter the mind.

The quieter the mind, the more obvious the Self.

When the mind unceasingly investigates its own nature, it discovers that it is a limited thing and that just behind the mind is all-knowingness.

As long as you are a part of, you are apart from the One.

Am is being. There is only one Beingness. I Am That I Am.

The word "I" is that number 1. All "I's" are one!

The first name for God is "I," your very Self.

Aloneness is Al-Oneness.

Lonesomeness is to the degree that you are separated from your Self.

Lose the sense of separateness and gain the sense of "I am All—every person, animal, and thing."

Every day is an opportunity to prove your mastership.

The realer Real is more in feelingness than it is in the hearing and seeing.

The five senses are in limitation. God, Truth, is in "feelingness in the heart." When the feelingness becomes matured, you will still see the world. But, instead of seeing it as separate and apart you will see it as your Self, You; that you are it and it is you! Then it becomes subjective rather than objective. You see it alright instead of all wrong.

This life of limitation is a reflection of the Real.

The only human thing about you is your belief that you are human. (You are Divine.) This belief is the medium for lack, sickness, limitation, and misery.

Love is a shove to the above.

Hate is a grate holding you down.

Help those who are not asking for it and get hurt.

Helping those who are not asking for it is imposing your will.

Helping one who is not asking for it is helping your ego.

We go in the wrong direction to learn what the right is.

Never get into a situation where you are helping someone spiritually and being hurt yourself. In the application of Truth, everyone gains.

Education teaches us things that are in the realm of limitation!

Get out of your cage. Be a sage.

We should get to the place where we feel that all mothers are our mothers, all fathers are our fathers, and all children are our children.

Language is an instrument of duality and admit separation. It implies the speaker, the one spoken to, and the matter spoken.

In Oneness language is useless as all is known.

Belief is accepting on hearsay.

Faith is stronger than belief.

Conviction is stronger than faith.

Knowing is absolute—there is no doubt.

Highest beauty is just beingness. Beauty is by attitude.

Seek without and you're in a bout.

Dive within and you'll thrive alive.

What comes out of a man's mouth is far more important than what goes into it.

If you want to know your consciousness, just look at who and what is around you.

Man is always down on what he is not up on.

A radical reliance on your Self (God) is the secret to the operation of the natural or divine law.

Acts performed with pure love build no future karma.

Karma is a gift of the gods of an opportunity to grow.

Fortunate is the one whom life does test, that he may grow. The greater the test, the greater one may grow.

Man's extremity is God's opportunity.

The closer one comes to the Self, the more beautiful everything becomes.

Inspirational delights are more delighting than other entertainment.

Inspiration is dipping into the realm of omniscience.

When your heart is in the right direction, your thinking is in the right direction.

Direct your attention toward the other one's beingness. (Take it off your little self, your ego.)

It is happier to love than to be loved.

It is happier to give than to be given.

Happiness is in the spirit of giving; not in the gift.

Anger in a hangar.

When there is a real spiritual vision, one is never left the same. He or she is left with a higher understanding and feeling of love.

One's outlook is determined by one's sight. To the physical eye, all is gross. To the mental eye, all is subtle. To the spiritual eye, there is only the Infinite Self, and everything becomes one infinitude.

In the waking state, the physical body perceives the manifold physical world. In dreaming sleep the mental body perceives the mental creations in their manifold forms and names. In deep dreamless sleep, no thing is perceived and the Self is.

The time required to accomplish the goal varies widely with individuals. Few accomplish it rapidly as few really accept the way. However everyone reaches it eventually.

Man can man the universe.

Die to death and you will be born into immortality.

See the world as a 3-ring circus, with yourself on the outside, observing and unaffected.

When reason and feeling agree, there is no more conflict within the individual.

You can help the world only to the degree you can help yourself.

Doingness is higher than havingness. Beingness is higher than doingness.

When the ego is strong enough, you can't see a locomotive coming at you.

Thoughts can actually dim the sun to one whose thoughts are dim.

For best decisions, decide only when your mind is quietest and when you feel happiest.

Keep Whole-ly company with Whole-ly thoughts.

We are at this moment the result of the sum of all our past thinking.

Advice is thievery. It deprives the other one of an opportunity to learn by his own doing.

When you offer a suggestion, take the attitude that the other one may accept it or not, as the other one wishes.

Pain turns off if you recognize it and feel it. Ninety percent of all pain is just memory of pain rather than pain, but it feels the same.

Grief is a thief.

Impatience is wanting things to be the way we want them to be—now!

Sympathy is feeling the misery of the other one and stepping down to where the other one is.

Compassion is understanding what a person is going through without feeling it and lending a hand to lift him up.

Body fatigue is a toxic condition caused by no love emotions.

If we have absolutely no conflicts, we never get tired.

The body has no intelligence to do—we do it.

Be untainted like the sainted.

We have free will to identify with the limited body or to identify with the unlimited self.

The joy that is ours is infinite. Joy is our inherent nature. Most people look for joys in the world, in people, and are disappointed.

Will without emotion for happiest results.

Will, in early childhood, is used to satisfy physical needs. In youth we have not yet learned to rightly direct it and it is blind will. In maturity we should direct it with wisdom into channels that fulfill the purpose of life.

It is the blind will of youth that causes juvenile delinquency.

When the will moves contrary to natural principle, there is immediately established an opposition to the wrong movement. When will moves in accord with natural principle it meets no resistance.

Will is a great accomplisher.

When you are happy, you don't have to invoke will, you just let things be.

Blame is accusative rather than corrective.

Misery is thinking of the things you do not want.

We die only to those around us, never to ourselves.

The greater the messenger shines, the less the message shines.

Understanding is that which stands under.

Tolerance implies ego.

Don't be little by belittling.

Seek the seeker. Find out who he is and you'll find God.

To be or not to be, that is the answer.

Miracles are not God. The source of miracles is God.

A miracle is done with knowingness. All it takes is a knowingness in your mind and it is done.

Consciousness is the sole composition of any thing.

Never accept responsibility for another one's behavior, even if that one be closely related. Allow him to grow through his own learning.

Intellectual discussion is a mental activity wherein thoughts, mostly of others, are kicked around. It avails no growth and is "spinning in circles." The only really useful mental activity is that which directs the mind toward the Self.

Opinion has nothing to do with Truth. Opinionating is wanting one's opinion accepted and therefore is wanting ego approval.

Opinionating is foisting one's thinking upon another. It is totally useless in finding Truth.

The mere recognizing of the problem is more than 50% of the solution, for no solution is possible if the problem is not recognized!

By running away from a problem, we only run into it in the future.

If you let life strike you, it will do so less cruelly than your imagination.

Scale of emotions from bottom to top—apathy, grief, fear, covert hostility, anger, indifference, acceptance, freedom, and joy.

Fear and it will appear. Quell the dwell on fear and it will disappear.

Any thinking or act that is "anti" (against) is non-acceptance and resistance. It is, therefore, not loving.

We are responsible for our own thinking.

Oneness is no-otherness.

I can have, I can be, I can do whatever I will or desire, because I am the infinite I Am expressing. (So long as I do not impose my will on others.)

SELF-GROWTH YARDSTICKS

We know only that which we can do. What can I do?

Am I completely at peace?

How loving am I? Do I love all beings?

> **THE WHOLE WORLD IS JUST A MERE THOUGHT— THINK OF THAT!**

Do I accept full responsibility for whatever happens to me?

Am I desireless? Do I have no attachments and no aversions?

Am I free to do or not to do the things I want or don't want to do?

Do I grant others their beingness?

Am I accepting of the world and the people around me?

Am I accepting of myself?

Am I completely free from reacting to people's wishes and thoughts?

Am I disturbed?

Am I able to express myself clearly, freely and truthfully?

Am I able to be alone and be at peace?

Is my life simple? (The further we are from the One, the more complex everything is.)

LAW OF COMPENSATION OR KARMA

Karma is the law of compensation. Whatever a man soweth, that shall he reap; that which a man thinks or does, returns to him in kind. Everything that one does now, causes the same thing to happen to one in the future. Likewise everything happening now, has its cause in something done in the past.

> **KARMA IS CAUSED BY DESIRES THAT REMAIN IN THE SUBCONSCIOUS MIND.**

Karma is destiny as it determines exactly what happens in life. We can do nothing in regard to all actions happening. Whatever has been destined to be done by us will be done by us.

If all our action is karmic and predestined, then our will that directs that action must necessarily be predestined.

However, we can conquer karma and destiny. There is free will—to identify with our body, or to identify with our real Self.

Do not identify with the body and be free from the pleasures and pains of the body and from the pleasant and unpleasant consequences of action. Identify with your real Self and remain eternally in the exalted state of supreme happiness.

A SUMMARY
THE SELF-GOD-ABSOLUTE TRUTH

Self (God) is Infinite, Limitless; One, Indivisible; Perfect; Changeless, Immutable; Timeless, Without Beginning or End; Whole, The All; Omniscient, Omnipotent, Omnipresent.

If God is All, that certainly must include us. If God is likened to the ocean and we to the drops in the ocean, then each drop has all the attributes and qualities of the whole ocean, that is, like the ocean, each drop is wet, fluid, salty, H2O, etc. If God is timeless and eternal, and if God is all, we are now, we always have been, and always will be that God which we are seeking. We are God ignorant of this fact, acting like not-God. All we need to do is improve our knowing of the fact that "I AM THAT I AM" until our knowledge is only that. Then we see and know that we are that which we have been seeking.

So the goal is to know that "I AM THAT I AM." This knowing, however, is not the intellectual knowing, which is but like a tape recording. This knowledge is an experienced knowledge gotten through Self realization, through stilling the five outer senses and concentrating the mind inwardly until the Self, Itself, gives us the answer by showing Itself.

No one can be taught Truth or God, each must realize Truth by himself or herself. A Teacher can give the direction, the way, and the pupil may take it.

All Truth is provable. Accept nothing on hearsay. Each must prove out everything for himself or herself.

There is only one Absolute Truth, and that is the Truth that is changeless. Before we attain to the one Absolute Truth we use the apparency of relative truth.

Reason and thinking, dealing with the limited senses, and being a lower level operation mind, cannot get us to the Absolute Truth, but must be used to get us in the direction of the Absolute Truth. Intuition, knowingness, super-consciousness reveal the Absolute Truth.

There are five major ways and paths suited to the various natures of man. The easiest way for most people today is through love and devotion to God. A second way is through serving mankind without interest in the fruits thereof. A third way is through use of intellect and wisdom. A fourth way is through mind control through breath control. The fifth way, Self Inquiry, is to pose the question, "Who am I?" until the answer presents itself.

Our rate of growth is directly proportional to the intensity of the desire for it.

Man thinks of himself as body, mind, and soul. Soul is the real Self—Infinite, All-Knowing, All-Powerful, Everywhere Present. Mind is a tool of Soul, used as an instrument to create and reflect the physical universe. Body is the creation of mind.

Therefore, we must first get to know that we are not the limited body, then that we are not the limited mind, and what is left is that we are the Pure Infinite Glorious Self, Omnipotent, Omniscient, and Omnipresent! This is the real evolution. Life, as we know it today, is in the limited realm of cause and effect. Natural or divine law works in accordance with cause and effect. To be masters and controllers of life, we need only to know that thinking is the cause and what ever happens in the physical world is the effect of that thinking! If, from this moment on, we would keep in mind only that which we want, that is only what we would get!

Remember, mind is only creative, and will create constructive and destructive things, determined by what we keep in mind!

"If you could stop thinking for one moment,

you would discover what you are."

Lester Levenson

LESTER IN HIS OWN WORDS

Thank you, Greetings and Love to each and every one of you. I think the biggest surprise tonight was to me. I didn't know I was going to talk until about 10 minutes before eight this evening, when I was told I was going to be the surprise.

So I began thinking, "What am I going to talk about? Talk about you, talk about me?" Then I realized, "What's the difference? We are all in the very same boat called life." We're all doing, in my eyes, the exact same thing that I did. We are all looking for the summum bonum. The highest good in the ultimate place. It is happiness, and we are without it all the time. Struggling for it, looking for it, wondering where it is?

Back in 1952, I claimed I found the place. It is right where I am. It is right where you are, and all this looking for it everywhere, every day year in and year out, is such a waste of time—when it is right where you are. We're all here in this classroom called earth, trying to discover something, the ultimate. And we are all looking for it externally where it isn't. If we would only turn our direction back upon ourselves, we would discover it right here, right where I am, right where you are, right in your very own being.

I say are you, you say yes. I say that's it. Do nothing else but that, and you will be in the ultimate state of happiness. So why don't you do it? You are so habituated in looking for it over there, over there in him, in her, in this job—and it is never there. So we are all going through the same trip of trying to discover what is this all about, where is my happiness, and when we stop chasing after it out there and we turn inward, we discover that all these hard negative, terrible feelings are only a feeling. And that it is possible to get rid of these feelings by releasing them. All these feelings are subconscious programs—every bit of them put in as prosurvival—it's not only fear, but survival. All our feelings have been programmed in to automatically keep us surviving. They keep looking out there, trying to survive, keeping our minds active subconsciously 24 hours a day, so never do we stop to think and discover what we are. If you could stop your thinking for one moment, you would go through the most tremendous experience that there is. That you are the totality of this universe in your beingness, that when your mind goes quiet, you will automatically see that—I am the most terrific being in this universe. I am whole, complete, and perfect. I always was, I am now and I always be.

So what is it that is keeping us from being in the most delectable state that there is? Simply the accumulated programs called feelings. All these negative feelings have us constantly struggling to survive, having us constantly struggling to survive, having us constantly looking away from this tremendous thing that we are, and all we need to do is quiet that mind and become self-obvious to ourselves of this tremendous being that we are.

How do we do it? I say it's simple. The Release® Technique. It happens to be the fastest, the most effective way there is to achieve this high state of being. When we are in total control of our universe, where every moment is a wonderful, wonderful moment, it is impossible to be unhappy. And I say that is our natural state when these negative feelings are released.

Some day you are going to do it. You are in the same boat where you are struggling, and you're doing everything to achieve that happiness, and some day you are going to get it because you will never stop until you get there. But if you want to do it faster, do it our way. I promise you will be very pleasantly surprised. Everything you are looking for is right where you are. All you need to do is to take off the blinders. Your vision is very blurred. You're looking through these subconscious programs—when you release them, your vision becomes clear and you discover you are the greatest. You're whole, you're complete, you're eternal. All your fear of dying disappears. And life is so comfortable after that, and there is no struggle, no struggle whatsoever, when you get these negative feelings up and out.

So I urge you to learn this technique. It's a tool, and in one week's time, there will be a big change in you for the better, and from there on, you will continue to get better and better, lighter and lighter, happier and happier.

This thing called love is your basic nature. All the love in the universe is in your basic nature. You will discover that happiness—your happiness—equates to your capacity to love, and conversely all your miseries equate to your need to be loved. Just love, love, love and you will be so happy and healthy and prosperous. But again, you need to lift out the non-love feelings. So again I urge you to try our way. I promise that you will be very satisfied. Try it, you will like it. Thank you so much for coming.

A few more words from

Lester Levenson

A MESSAGE FROM LESTER

So we have had a chance to talk heart to heart. I hope this has helped you. And I want you to know there is much more help available. I have talked to you in a manner that is designed to provoke thinking that leads you to a new realization. I have talked to you in a way that attempts to reach the part of you that inherently and intuitively understands more than your intellect. All this leads you to wisdom. Wisdom that is higher than intellectual knowledge.

If you have found these words of value, I suggest you go on and explore the do-it-yourself method I have developed that will show you how to increase your understanding every day. It is called the Release® Technique. It will give you keys to self-growth and allow you to keep it going from here on. The Release Technique is based on the premise that each one of us has no limits except those that we hold onto subconsciously, and when we let go of our subconscious limitations, we discover that our potential is unlimited. Unlimited in the direction of health, happiness, affluence and materiality. The Release Technique will help you achieve the kind of life you want and even more importantly, it will assist you in achieving self-realization.

The Release Technique is kind of a post-graduate course to this book. Practice it and achieve the ultimate state.

APPENDIX A

LESTER'S RELEASE TECHNIQUE COURSE
WILL HELP YOU

- Rid yourself of attachments and aversions.

- Feel love any time.

- Discover the truth of your being.

- Awaken to your true nature.

- Have inner transformation.

- Clear away years of accumulated confusion.

- Have abundance in every way.

- Manifest your dreams into reality.

- Rid yourself of worry.

- Access answers from your higher self.

HERE'S HOW PEOPLE THAT USE LESTER'S "THE RELEASE® TECHNIQUE" HAVE MORE ABUNDANCE WITH EASE

"The most pronounced, tangible evidence that I'm getting, only through using the method, is in the monetary aspects of my business. I'm on a commission basis only, and I've earned as much in the first quarter of this year as I did in all of last year."

Karen Brock, CA
President, Brock Enterprises

"I took The Release Technique because I was under a lot of business and personal pressure. I find now that I'm more relaxed, easier in all my relationships and making a lot more money with much less effort—playing smarter, not harder."

Tom Beyers, AZ
Senior Vice President, First Federal Mortgage Company

"My business has tripled since learning the Abundance Course, yet I'm spending most of my time traveling and having fun all the time. The Technique is so powerful, I've had my entire family learn the Technique. I also got rid of 20 years of asthma. Last month I made over 1 million dollars using this Technique."

Jim Whitman, World Traveler

"I have regained my focus on abundance thanks to The Abundance Course. Customers are calling me to advertise on my radio show—big time! I recommend it to all who want abundance, riches, success, happiness and health. It really does work."

Jacquie Solomon, AZ
Radio Hostess, KFNX

"I'm excited!" I have already made over $7,000 and I am working on a deal now I expect to triple that…Anyone can do it. All that the Abundance course claims is true and then some. I can't imagine everyone not taking this course."

Kathy Shoden, CA
Sales and Marketing

"I just completed the Abundance Course for the first time last weekend. On the second day, I received an offer for a house I have been trying to sell for three years. Before the course ended, I received three offers on the house. My sales results have been amazing—I've had the biggest month I ever had, and that's just in one week! I can't imagine anyone not wanting to learn The Easy Way."

Gayle Henderson, AZ
Russ Lyon Realty Co.

VAST ABUNDANCE IS WITHIN YOU...
WHY NOT JOIN IN ON THE FUN?

HAVE ABUNDANT HEALTH

"I took the Abundance Course to have more financial abundance in my life. Not only did I get that big time, but I had chronic pain in my jaw for 6 years. I was able to get rid of it the very first evening of practicing The Technique. My golf improved, I lowered my score by 14 points in two weeks. This course is worth millions—Don't wait. Call them right now!"

Roger Brunnetti, CA
Marketing Consultant

I have had a full recovery from a boating accident since taking the course. I did not have full range-of-motion in my left arm, I do now and I have been able to stop taking 14 different pills."

Raul Marmol, CA

"During the second day, I worked on an injured foot that had been bothering me for years. I was wearing a bandage and a sandal. The next day I was able to wear shoes and it didn't hurt me at all! I'm not angry at anyone, and I like myself more, and I feel joy all the time. Wow!"

Cathryn Willmeng, AZ
Real Estate Appraiser

"I let go of a lower back pain I had been suffering with for a long time during the third day of the course. I even took off my back support—WOW, what a course."

Gary Sylvester, CA
Telecommunications

BE IN TOTAL CONTROL OF YOUR LIFE

"On Sunday morning (during the course), I woke up with the knowledge that I had found the tools that empower me to take back control of my life, and that's not a goal— that's a fact."

Linda Carella, CA
V.P. Marketing, Tova Corp.

"Acceptance expanded, trust expanded, love expanded, freedom is and continuously unfolds easily! I also received five checks in the mail yesterday—and money and joy just keep rolling in. I also have a major art show this week at the Scottsdale Art Center and it just happened with ease."

Monica Martinez, AZ
artist

"This course helped me bring back the value of more consistent releasing. It has given me the awareness to use the tools I have for releasing with ease. Thank you for putting such a practical spin on the method. My life is so much richer for having use of the tools and Lester's wisdom."

Rosalie Lurie, CA, Fundraiser

"I no longer judge myself and others. I no longer feel guilty about anything; I love myself and others. I'm experiencing peace and joy more and more. I can't imagine anyone not taking this fabulous course."

Scott Jones, CA
Advertising Executive

"I gained the ability to stop being counterproductive in my life. I can now erase any attitude of 'I never win.' It enabled me to take control of myself–wow!"

Kathy Mullen, CA

RID YOURSELF OF FAILURE HABITS

"I actually let go of beating myself up—I hadn't thought it was possible. I feel exhilarated and energetic after years of fatigue. I have more clarity and peace and improved self confidence—I have a feeling of 'I can' after years of depressions and anxiety—Thank you Lester and Larry."

Luz Ugalde Fortner, CA

"I've taken many lessons, but it wasn't until I took The Release Technique that I really, really got on track. Wow–I really didn't know what I was missing! Releasing is the greatest, and our natural way…Don't miss this opportunity."

Ron Hamady, CA, Movie Producer

RID YOURSELF OF FEAR AND GAIN CLARITY

I unlocked my fear, lack and scarcity feelings that stopped me from having abundance for years. It was powerful and fun and easy. I can't imagine anyone not taking this course—it's a must."

Joseph Harrington, CA
Psychologist

"My clarity in life improved dramatically. I see where I am and where to go next. My abundance improved just in that one weekend—I wish all could attend."

Craig Davis, Winnetka, CA, School Psychologist

"I had severe anxiety when I would get on the freeway. It was preventing me from having a life. Then I took The Abundance Course. On the first day, I dumped the phobia. It was so simple that it was almost hard to believe it could be so easy! I now look at life in such a way that it becomes magical. I recommend it to all."

Lauren Brent, CA
Esthetician

"I was able to retire from a job I had for years, and I feel terrific about it! I'm using the 'Butt' system and it works. Thank you, the course is the greatest."

Charles Jones, Washington, DC
Psychotherapist

"I released about worrying about the future. My life really works!"

Bebe Young, CA
Businesswoman

"I just completed The Abundance Course. My understanding gets clearer and clearer. My decision process is fantastic, and I'm having fun all the time. My business has tripled, and I have more time to do what I want. It's easy—anyone can do it."

Judy Smith Whitman, AZ
Art Dealer

FEEL LOVE ANYTIME YOU WANT

"These past few weeks have been especially wonderful—'Joyous' is the true word. More and more I do see myself as one with everything. Right now, Larry, I feel as if I'm going to explode with joy—and I can't stop laughing! All is well! All should join in on the fun."

Clara Sida-McCoy, AZ
Housewife/Secretary

"The new work that is being done on abundance is fantastic. I'm just busting with happiness and doing and having what I want all the time."

Cecilia Gallagher, AZ
Business Developer

"I never thought I could feel this good about myself. I now have a tool I can use each day of my life."

Yvonne Medina, CA
Client Service Genetics Institute

UNLOCK WHAT'S HOLDING YOU BACK FROM HAVING TOTAL ABUNDANCE AND JOY IN YOUR LIFE—ONCE AND FOR ALL LEARN TO TRUST YOURSELF

"By the end of Day 2, I achieved a sense of deep calm. While driving home, I found I wasn't so irritated by other drivers and I remained unperturbed. My boyfriend commented on the youthful, lighter look on my face over dinner."

Kim LaChance, CA
Therapist

"I have been going through books and seminars for so long. This course allowed me to see that life can be without problems. The future is wonderful now."

Pirayeh Shaban, CA
Coordinator

IMPROVE RELATIONSHIPS

"I am able to release my anger at my girlfriend whenever she gets angry/jealous about our relationship. Our relationship has greatly improved in a short time."

Jay Torres, CA
Salesman

"My relationship with my children has greatly improved. I am able to handle disgruntled clients without being uptight. I lost my craving for smoking and stopped smoking in the first day of the course."

Thomas Mitchel, CA
Investment Advisor

"Everything is working for me with ease—my relationships are getting better, my business is exploding with ease, abundance just is and it's easy!"

Shawna Leach-Lugo, AZ
Artist

"I can allow myself to love people for who they are, no matter what."

John Cullen, IL
Contractor

MORE REPORTS FROM ABUNDANCE COURSE GRADUATES WHO HAVE DROPPED UNWANTED HABITS

"A few weeks after learning The Release Technique, I completely stopped my chain smoking habit and the craving hasn't come back in 15 years since stopping."

Don Janklow, CA
President, Janklow & Associates

"I have learned to relax by releasing, and an unexpected gain has been that I no longer have a desire for alcohol—it feels good."

Jack Dimalante, NY

"I lost five pounds during the first week of the course without thinking about it!"

Lloyd Scott, TX

"I used this method when I was feeling hunger, and I no longer feel the desire to eat."

Rita Recken, OH

ELIMINATE STRESS

"Sleeping better than I have in years. I quit taking drugs for my arthritis and feel better without them."

Raymond Hanson, CA

"I connected with the ease of releasing. I simply didn't know how much resistance I had. By Sunday, I had so much energy it was great and after only four hours of sleep. I feel lighter and happier."

Ariana Attie, CA
Legal Secretary

"The first weekend I discovered my feeling of fatigue could be alleviated, and I drove 200 miles without the sleepiness and feeling of heaviness that so often plagued me."

Ruth A. Riegel, Chicago, IL

"I had several physical ailments including migraine headaches, diverticulitis, gout and severe hypoglycemia, and the week after taking the course was scheduled for surgery. But within a few days after beginning to release, the surgical condition disappeared and never re-appeared. My other physical problems cleared up. I believe these good effects are due to the stress reduction brought about by using the Method."

Dr. David Hawkins, NY
Medical Director, The North Nassau Mental Health Center

"I think it is becoming evident, in my observation, that the techniques learned in the program were beneficial to people who work under the stress and strain that we do in the Investment Banking Industry. I have personally benefited, especially when I ran the New York City Marathon shortly after an illness."

Thomas J. Kitrick
Vice President Training and Development
Goldman, Sachs & Co.

40-year Search is Over

"Over the last 40 years, I have spent thousands of dollars and invested hundreds of hours in an uncountable number of seminars, courses and techniques. I purchased The Abundance Course hoping, as always, that I had finally found something that would work. I did! Now my reactions to events during the day are much more positive than ever before. Wow!"

Bill Cook, OK

Multimillionaire Heals Heart

"I am a multimillionaire who has learned how to attract money easily into my life via the route to real estate development. What I had not known was that it is okay to enjoy my work and it is okay to enjoy spending the fruits of my labor. I am now able to tithe and gift and spend my money joyfully and peacefully. What a difference The Abundance Course made in this miraculous turnaround of attitude for me. Further, my heart used to hurt and the doctors would consistently tell me it is fine. My heart no longer hurts me–I've released, it's free."

Robert White, MA

Triples Income

"Thank you for your wonderful "Abundance" tapes. After listening to your tapes a thought popped into my mind that increased my income 3 times. I evaluate children (I'm a consulting school psychologist) at a rate of $350/evaluation–write up reports and type them on a computer–formerly one evaluation a day. I now do three evaluations (takes 11/2 hrs. per evaluation), tape my reports and have the school secretary type them up. My income is now over $1,000/day and I work only 2 days a week. I have more leisure time to do other things that give me joy. Again, thanks to you and the works of Lester Levenson–a truly great man. "

Dr. Samuel L. Beitchman, Ph.D., NJ

Joy Spilling Out

"The Abundance Course is truly the marvel of life. I am a skeptical person (or I was!) and I didn't think the course would do much for me, but now I am a believer—actually I know that this course is the key to happiness with no sorrow. Right now, I feel absolutely joyous—it's spilling out of me—and it's for the best reason, which is no reason at all.

I'd like to thank you for your everlasting patience, love and givingness that Lester shared with us."

Foster Brown, MA

Happy all the Time and Makes $100,000 in One Week

"The Abundance Course just got me much clearer about my life. It showed me how to have a positive attitude all the time. I'm now happy all the time and the joy is just bubbling up. Because I'm even so much more positive now, I was able to make $100,000 last week in the stock market."

Sarit Majhor, NM

Happiest Time in His Entire Life

"After ordering and receiving the home study version of The Abundance Course, I allowed it to sit on the shelf for several months. Then one day I simply decided to follow the instructions and do it on a daily basis. That was about 3 months ago, and what a journey it has been. Traditionally my medical practice slows down the first quarter of the year for various reasons and picks up in the spring. Amazingly, I have had the most productive January I've had in many years, and continues into February. In fact, January was the second most productive month I have had in twelve months. Not only that, something in a profound way has happened to my attitude toward my patients and life in general. I feel so much love toward my patients and about everyone else. It's really weird. I have come to the conclusion that I just may be the happiest I have ever been in my entire life. That's not bad for a person who previously thought he was just an old, worn-out Doc."

Dr. Clyde Shreve, UT

Oneness and Bliss

"I cannot express the extent of my gratitude for the wisdom you imparted to me this past weekend. The Abundance Course was beyond anything I could have imagined– indeed it finally gave me an experience that I had been searching for 19 years. I picked up a book on Zen Buddhism at the time I have been searching for the experience described in that book and the many, many others I have read since that time. I have tried various techniques since that time including intensive medication, Tony Robbins, etc. but it wasn't until I was driving home from The Abundance Course (driving down a Los Angeles freeway no less) that I had an experience of Oneness and Bliss. I finally have found the way out of the feeling of separateness and pain that comes with living a normal human life. This is priceless knowledge and timeless wisdom."

Sonny Ritscher, CA

Overcomes Sadness Easily

"In September 1994, my youngest son, Matt, age 21, was killed in an auto accident and for these seven years I lived in grief. Though the pain eased over the years I could hardly speak his name without breaking down. I completed The Abundance Course at the end of October and last week released on Matt's death. I felt like someone had lifted a boulder off my back. The empty, squeezing, tightness in my chest was gone. I felt wonderful, so to see how much I'd release I watched a home video. Seeing Matt I felt only love and happiness. (No more tears, no more pain.) Yesterday I even talked to a friend about the accident and did not get upset in the least. This is a tremendous gain for me and I recommend this course to everyone.

Thank you so much!"

Jeri Von Wolff, IA

M.D.'s Health Improves

"My allergies have improved significantly since using The Abundance Course. I used to have really bad neck and back tension and that has improved significantly as well. I am more at peace with regard to my relationships with my parents. My ability to treat patients has improved and I feel better able to tune-in with what's going on with others. I recommend the course to anyone who wants to improve their life in every way."

Clara Hsu, M.D., CA

Books and Audios for Your Personal Growth

The Power of Love

Book by Lester Levenson

Lester speaks about love in a way you have never heard.

Item #1039 $20.00 plus $5.00 shipping*

The Abundance Book

Comes with 2 bonus audios

The Abundance Course has now been published in book form. It's a terrific way to Supercharge your Releasing skills.

This Exciting Book Will Help You:

- Reinforce and Supercharge your Releasing
- Have long-term financial success
- Deal calmly with world events regardless of what the media says
- Have inner calmness in the midst of pressure
- Propel yourself to new heights of joy and fulfillment
- Have vibrant health and energy

Item #1015T / #1015-CD $65 plus $12.95 shipping*

No Attachments, No Aversions

Book

Lester tells his own story in his very own words. In the margin are Lester's own notes in his own handwriting. Each time you read it you will discover something profound that will help you in your own personal quest toward freedom.

Item #1012 $25.00 plus $5.00 shipping*

In Retreat with Lester Levenson

Audios

This dynamic three-audio set of Lester Levenson was recorded live at several Nine-Day Retreats in the 1980s. These audios are full of practical suggestions on how to accelerate your releasing for freedom. They also contain rare accounts of Lester describing his personal experience of freedom.

Item #1007-T/#1007-CD $39.95 plus $6.00 shipping*

The Way with Lester Levenson

Audios

Three audio programs of Lester Levenson recorded in 1989. Lester was pulling no punches as he spoke with a small, dedicated group of staff at the Retreat Center. These rare recordings contain powerful pointers on how to achieve freedom now. This three audio set includes a bonus audio recorded in 1973.

Item #1006-T/#1006-CD $39.95 plus $6.00 shipping*

A Fireside Chat with Lester Levenson – Audios

We all have many questions that we would love to ask Lester. Hear Lester answering puzzling questions from graduates.

Audio 1—Looking for Happiness
Audio 2—Attachments and Aversions
Audio 3—Communication and Love
Audio 4—About Releasing

Item #1024-T / #1024-CD $39.95 plus $6.00 shipping*

The Ultimate Goal—Volume I – Audios

Audio 1 —The Ultimate Truth; Experiencing Truth
Audio 2—Letting Go of Ego
Audio 3—The Mind Mirror
Audio 4—Creating All You Desire
Audio 5—Silence, Love and Grace
Audio 6—The Key to Individual Freedom

Item #1005-T   #1005-CD $79.95 plus $8.00 shipping*

The Ultimate Goal—Volume II – Audios

Audio 1—Happiness is Love
Audio 2—The Source of All Intelligence
Audio 3—The Answer is Here All the Time
Audio 4—There Are No Problems
Audio 5—The Steps to Being What You Are
Audio 6—Beingness

Item #1008-T / #1008-CD $79.95 plus $8.00 shipping*

Private Lessons with Lester – Audios

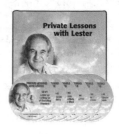

How would you like to be taught, privately, about Releasing by Lester? Recently we have obtained, newly found Lester audio's recorded in 1986. Lester was recorded teaching graduates how to go deeper into Releasing. You will be astounded and inspired as you listen to Lester talking at his very best.

Audio 1 –Lester on Letting Go of Resisting Freedom
Audio 2 –You Can Do Anything
Audio 3 –You Are Not the Body or The Mind
Audio 4 –Going Free
Audio 5 –No Limitations
Audio 6 –The Ultimate Freedom

Item #1042-CD $89.95 plus $8.00 shipping*

How to Order Today

CA residents please add sales tax (8.25%).

Order by Phone:
1-888-333-7703 Toll-free (24 hours a day)
Outside U.S. call 1-541-957-4969
Toll-free Canada, Hawaii, Alaska: 1-877-472-3317

Order by Fax:
1-757-301-3646

Order by Mail:
Release Technique, LP
2800 Crusader Circle, Suite 10
Virginia Beach, VA 23453

Order from our Secure Web Site:
www.releaseTechnique.com

All Credit Cards Accepted

Total value of **over $3,000** *for a limited time*

❑ **Yes!** Please rush me the **Abundance Course** Home Study audio set so I may examine it risk-free for 30 days.

❑ **Yes!** I read THE ULTIMATE TRUTH BOOK, so I qualify for the specialprice of $269. I save **$226** off the regular price of $495.

❑ **Yes!** I also qualify for the **5 free audios**, a **$125** value, mine to keep even if I return the material for a full refund.
(Less shipping and handling, of course.)

❑ Please rush me **CDs**.

❑ Enclosed is $281.95 ($269 plus $12.95 U.S. for shipping and handling)
(Overseas orders $316.95 U.S.—$269 plus $47.95 shipping and handling)
CA residents please add $21.19 (8.25%) sales tax. Total = $303.14
Sorry, we do not accept C.O.D. orders.

Make checks payable to Release Technique, LP

Total _____   ❑ Check ❑ Visa ❑ MasterCard

Your discount code is UT-2.   ❑ Discover ❑ American Express

For fast action, call toll-free (24 hours a day): 1-888-333-7703

Name _____

Address _____City_____State____Zip_____

Phone (day) _____ (eve.) _____
(In case we need to contact you if there is a question about your order.)

E-mail _____Occupation _____

Credit Card # _____ Expiration Date _____

Signature _____
Please be sure to check your address carefully and indicate any corrections.

Release Technique, LP
2800 Crusader Circle, Suite 10, Virginia Beach, VA 23453

DOUBLE GUARANTEE
If I am not convinced that the Abundance Course will work for me I may:
1) Receive Free coaching over the telephone, or 2) Return the course
within 30 days for a prompt refund and still keep the 5 free bonus audios.
(Less shipping and handling, of course.)